D1758023

The Emma Press
Anthology of Motherhood

'*The Emma Press Anthology of Motherhood* is a fantastic
anthology. [...] It is not schmaltz, it is one of the most
powerful collections I have ever had the pleasure of reading.'
– Wendy Pratt, *Northern Soul*

'How delightful [...] to pick up a book that collects
many talented female poets together, to describe a part
of the female experience that, though not quintessential
in terms of the feminist narrative, remains uniquely
feminine and still provokes enormous debate whenever
it is mentioned in the mainstream media.'
– Alisande Fitzsimons, *For Books' Sake*

Other titles from the Emma Press

POETRY ANTHOLOGIES

Campaign in Poetry: The Emma Press Anthology of Political Poems
The Emma Press Anthology of Dance
Slow Things: Poems about Slow Things
The Emma Press Anthology of Age
Mildly Erotic Verse
Urban Myths and Legends: Poems about Transformations
The Emma Press Anthology of the Sea

POETRY ANTHOLOGIES FOR CHILDREN

Falling Out of the Sky: Poems about Myths and Monsters
Watcher of the Skies: Poems about Space and Aliens
The Head that Wears a Crown: Poems about Kings and Queens

POETRY COLLECTIONS FOR CHILDREN

Moon Juice, by Kate Wakeling
The Noisy Classroom, by Ieva Flamingo (Jul '17)

THE EMMA PRESS PICKS

The Held and the Lost, by Kristen Roberts
Captain Love and the Five Joaquins, by John Clegg
Malkin, by Camille Ralphs
DISSOLVE to: L.A., by James Trevelyan
The Dragon and the Bomb, by Andrew Wynn Owen (Jan '17)

POETRY PAMPHLETS

True Tales of the Countryside, by Deborah Alma
AWOL, by John Fuller and Andrew Wynn Owen
Goose Fair Night, by Kathy Pimlott
Trouble, by Alison Winch
Mackerel Salad, by Ben Rogers

THE EMMA PRESS
Anthology of
Motherhood

Edited by Rachel Piercey and Emma Wright

With poems from Deborah Alma, Stephanie Arsoska,
Liz Berry, Sara Boyes, Carole Bromley, Laura Chalar,
George David Clark, Flora de Falbe, Kate Garrett, Hilary
Gilmore, Melinda Kallasmae, David Kennedy, Anna Kirk,
Anna Kisby, Peter LaBerge, Eve Lacey, Anna Leader,
Marena Lear, Katherine Lockton, Rachel Long, Julie
Maclean, Ikhda Ayuning Maharsi, Kathryn Maris,
Richard O'Brien, Rachel Piercey, Clare Pollard, Jacqueline
Saphra, Kathryn Simmonds, Lavinia Singer, Catherine
Smith, Camellia Stafford and Megan Watkins

Illustrated by Emma Wright

THE EMMA PRESS

THE EMMA PRESS

First published in Great Britain in 2014
by the Emma Press Ltd

Reprinted in 2016

Poems copyright © individual copyright holders 2014
Selection copyright © Rachel Piercey and Emma Wright 2014
Introduction copyright © Emma Wright 2014
Illustrations copyright © Emma Wright 2016

ISBN 978-0-9574596-7-0

A CIP catalogue record of this book
is available from the British Library.

Printed and bound in Great Britain
by TJ International, Padstow.

The Emma Press
theemmapress.com
queries@theemmapress.com
Birmingham, UK

Contents

PART 3

PART 4

Introduction

The Emma Press Anthology of Motherhood is not a comfortable book. It houses many disparate voices and offers no easy resolution to the tensions of expectation between women and motherhood, and mothers and children. Generally, the most joyful poems are about pregnancy and the most conflicted poems concern adult women and their mothers. Devotion often leads to reproach in poems about difficult mothers, and the personal cost of such a biological and emotional capacity is questioned as much as it is validated.

Despite this, *The Emma Press Anthology of Motherhood* is not a downbeat book. There are notes of contentment chiming alongside the notes of exhaustion, and resentment and doubt often co-exist with tenderness and sympathy. I think the challenges to the traditional maternal mainstays of selflessness and unconditional love strengthen them and, better still, reconstruct them in kinder, more forgiving ways. Over the course of the book, a picture emerges of a different kind of Madonna figure: one whose capacity to love is equalled by and not at all diminished by her capacity to feel the strain and wish the whole role away.

When Rachel Piercey and I were planning this anthology, we discussed at length how we wanted to portray mothers and motherhood. We wanted to produce a book which commented on motherhood as a social state as well as the experience of being and having a mother, and we wanted it to reflect as wide a range of views as possible, the prevailing tone being one of sympathy and compassion. We hoped to represent motherhood in a way that was fair and clear-eyed – celebratory in parts, but not sentimentalised. We were fortunate that our call for submissions and description of the kind of book we hoped to create seemed to strike a chord with writers across the world, so we were able to find exactly the poems we needed.

The final selection turned out sadder than I had expected, but it felt true to the major preoccupations of all the poets in the pool of submissions, just as it felt important to acknowledge the most testing expectations and conflicts encountered by people in relation to motherhood. I could not be happier with the poems we were able to collect, and I hope we have achieved our goal of producing a nuanced picture of mothers and motherhood. The poems in this book are truthful, honest, loving, compassionate, heartfelt, humane, thought-provoking, brutal and defiant. Individually, they are powerful and moving, but as a collection they work together to create a vision of motherhood at once terrible and magnificent – which is, I think, fair.

Emma Wright
WINNERSH
February 2014

Part 1

On Returning a Child to her Mother at the Natural History Museum

Hello, my name is Kathryn and I've come
here to return your daughter, Emily.
She told me you'd suggested that she look
around upstairs in 'Earthquakes and Volcanoes',
then meet you and her brothers in the shop.
You know that escalator leading to
the orb? It's very long and only goes
one way, you can't turn round. She asked me if
I knew the way back down and would we come
with her into the earthquake simulator –
that reproduction of the grocery shop
in Kobe, where you see the customers
get thrown around with Kirin beer and soy
sauce, things like that. She told us stuff about
your family. Apparently you had
a baby yesterday! That can't be right:
you're sitting here without one and my God
your stomach's flat! She also said she'd had
an operation in the hospital
while you were giving birth one floor below.
I know, I know: kids lie and get confused,
mine do that too. She talks a lot. She's fat.
She may not be an easy child to love.
I liked her, though. I liked her very much,
and having her was great, the only time
all day my daughter hasn't asked me for

a dog! We got downstairs and funnily
enough we found your middle son. He ran
to us upset and asked us where you were.
But here you are – exactly where you said –
the shop! Don't worry: I don't ever judge
a mother. Look at me: my daughter drank
the Calpol I left out when she was two;
I gave my kids Hundreds and Thousands once
for dinner while I lay down on the floor,
a wreck. I know you well! Here's Emily.

All My Mad Mothers

My mother gathered every yellow object she could find:
daffodils and gorgeous shawls, little pots of bile and piles
of lemons. One day we caught her with a pair
of fishnet stockings on a stick, trying to catch the sun.

My mother never travelled anywhere without her flippers,
goggles and a snorkel. She'd strip at any opportunity:
The Thames, The Serpentine, the shallows of a garden pond,
a puddle in the park. She was no judge of depth.

My mother was a dipterologist, sucking fruit flies through a straw.
Our house was filled with jars of corpses on display.
Sometimes she'd turn them out, too dead to flee, their wings
still glinting, make them into chokers for our party bags.

My mother barely spoke between her bruises:
her low-cut gown was tea-stained silk. From behind
her Guccis or Versaces, she would serve us salty dinners,
stroke a passing cheek, or lay her head on any waiting shoulder.

My mother was an arsonist. She kept a box of matches
in her bra, lined up ranks of candles, ran her pretty fingers
through the flames. At full moon, she would drag
our beds into the garden, set them alight and howl.

My mother was a fine confectioner. We'd come upon her sponges,
softly decomposing under sweaters in a drawer, or oozing
sideways in a filing cabinet. Once, between her pearls and
emerald rings, we found a maggot gateau, iced with mould.

———————

My mother was so hard to grasp: once we found her in a bath
of olive oil, or was it sesame, her skin well-slicked.
She'd stocked the fridge with lard and suet, butter: salted
and unsalted, to ease her way into this world. Or out of it.

FLORA DE FALBE

This, then, is how you should pray

My mother,
who is upstairs editing bathroom catalogues,
you have taken back your name.
For too long it languished in the attic,
outdated as your first party frock;
you shook it out of its binbag.
It smelled of mothballs and dried lavender.
Now that you are older and blonder
spring will come: the worst is done,
and you wear your old jacket of a name
as the '90s creep back into fashion.
In a year I will leave you
for the bright lights of a provincial sky;
so give me my daily bread
and I will hold you
as you held me
my mother –
yours are the bathroom catalogues
and the whole of a glorious future.

National Moth Night

The story goes: I'm six or so and stamping
on endangered moths, to your embarrassment
and the shock of members of the Wildlife Watch.
Before or afterwards we stayed up late for badgers,
and you picked me up from parties where I drank
too much and kept you up past twelve, with work at nine.
It's different now – the dogs forget my name,
and sheets are changed, and furniture gets rearranged
without my knowledge. Now I wake up late,
skip breakfast, never call, and when you visit
all the mugs are stained and you swear you can see my bones.
And I am still a passenger, hungover, overdrawn,
winding the window down and talking in abbreviations.
Only sometimes do I know how much you carry me.
You steer, and let me talk at last about the six months
sieved through a butterfly net, and the engine chokes
at a roundabout; the seatbelt presses down my chest
like a walking boot on a white gauze sheet.
We're changing gear. I always did forget.

The worlds

My mum made us many worlds
overlapping in bright circles,
and made us the shape-shifting shoes
to stride into them.

She made England
and she made Australians,
mouths filled with eucalyptus phrases;

she made shop-owners,
plying our biscuits and lemonade
to ramblers in our lane

and she made ramblers,
free from the hard charm of destination.

She made an artist's daughters,
story-hearers and selective believers.
She made tree-dwellers,
trend-leavers and fancy-dress-wearers,

irregular pegs. She made the round holes
shimmy, she made silly,
she made kindness, she made calm.

My mum makes us the world
as wide as the world
and as small as the circle of her arms.

My Mother Moves Into Adolescence

My mother comes round with my star signs,
a thin apple pie, shop-bought
that no-one will want and the *Daily Mail*.
We say thank you,
the boys kiss her and go upstairs.

She presents me with six things:

1. *You must sort out breakdown for my car Debbie,
because my English is bad.*
I get the leaflet, circle the right policy, hand it back to her.

2. *Where must I buy new front door?*
I say B&Q? Homebase? I said that before Mum.
She waits for me to offer to measure it and take her.
I put the kettle on.

3. *Where do I find man to fit new door?*
I tell her I don't know Mum,
Look in Yellow Pages?
She waits for me to get the Yellow Pages.
I get her a piece of cake with her tea.
Just a thin piece... chorti... chorti.
She eats a large piece, noisily.

4. *Where do I find man to fit carpet?*
Yellow Pages Mum?
Where do I look under?
Carpet fitters Mum.

5. *You must show me where to write e-mail to Aleem.*
I show her.

6. *I need you write letter to estate agent.*
I can't do it today Mum.
You are so lazy Debbie, she screams.
All her rage spits out.
She throws her mug into the sink and it shatters there.

I liked that green mug with the spots,
from Woolworths.
There is no more Woolworths.
Suddenly,
terribly, unbearably sad
that there is no more Woolworths,
I tell her to go and never come back.

Dreams of Falling

My mami wraps me in an *aguayo*,
packs me into its colours as tightly
as mince meat tucked into an *empanada*.
She pulls up her *pollera*, then throws
me from my aunt's seventh floor window.
She does this because I'll fall anyway.

I am alone with only an open window
and seven floors to fall for company.
I am falling towards my brother in London.
I am falling for the sweet-seller's baby.
I am following her down the street as I fall.
I am as small as my mother's black doll
whose head broke off and never got fixed.

I will always always never not fall.

Lipstick

My Mother always said lipstick
was for whores, or
for special occasions,
which didn't come around often
because hers stayed in her top drawer, waiting.

'Just nick it, she'll never notice,' my sister would say.
But in her room God
was always watching, peeling
at the corners above the bed, slightly left-aligned,
the side Dad used to sleep on.

This and These

A word said slant, the weight of an island
obstructing her tongue
at the checkout, inciting
a salacious grin from the clerk
who let her anguish continue
flushed with power
until a final pronunciation
of her pronunciation, a grandiose
gesture of acceptance, allowed her to smile
(a turn of features like a perfectly
executed ballroom spin)
and soften her grip on my small hand.
I, then about six or seven,
remember thinking that he had probably
never seen a smile so beautiful
nor ever would again, as we strode out
into the parking lot, hand in hand
stepping over fast food wrappers
my mother speaking lightly to me
with the ocean-wide, rolling barrel vowels
musical rests and holds
of our language
the wind beneath the sails of Spanish ships
rustling somewhere in her hair.

Madame de Grignan Writes to the Marquise

Mother, I'm stifled under your love.
Your letters jump at me, shout behind my skirts,
tug at my puffed sleeves.
Ma bonne, they cry, *you haven't written,*
I tremble from head to foot,
sleep has deserted me and so has reason.
Do you not know, the black ink screams,
how much I love you? It's as if my heart and soul
were being torn from me. Mother, two hundred leagues
    between us
and my rooms still throb with anguish. I am weighed down
by my *grossesse* and your sorrow.
Will I die in childbirth? You went distracted
when I almost drowned in the Rhône. But I'd stood against
the wind, seen the stark ruined arches charge forward,
    felt a strange
joyfulness buoy me over the grey waters.
I end now. M. de Grignan
embraces you. I enclose
a gift of gloves for your fine hands.

The Marquise de Sévigné is famous for the charming letters she wrote to her
daughter, Mme de Grignan, living far away from her mother after her marriage
to a nobleman from Provence. They corresponded for nearly thirty years, and the
Marquise de Sévigné worried endlessly about her daughter's health. In early 1671,
Mme de Grignan almost died while trying to cross the river Rhône in a boat. A
strong wind pushed the boat towards a collapsed bridge's arches, and a fatal crash
was barely avoided. She was perhaps pregnant at the time – although not heavily
so, as in the poem, since her child was only born in November of that year.

Poem for Virgin Starfish

In Polaroids
faces drowning my mother

I would drown for you, Jonah.
Would you like to go to the sea?

Mother I am in the sea now I am praying
now beyond the low tide mark pinned under
men gripping virgin starfish in their fingers I would
be
more beautiful less drowning with a mother not
a bible shaped woman to call my name

Would you like to go to the sea?
Jonah, be what your mother named.

The nature of tides entering my body pinching
unforgettable nerves like brine I have promised
myself a new mother to soothe the surface protect
from men I thought were tides who made the whole
atlantic orgasm call *yeah baby yeah* mouth frothing
something holy wanting full of color never drowning

M

After a long time looking, after making no connections,
after seeing you from time to time last summer,
after calling you drunk, bad mother, bad… At a time

when leaves fluttered everywhere in the park
and paths pounded to the revolution of buggy wheels. After all this,
despite myself I have threaded my way,

I have blown up coloured glass to magnify you in.
You, who were drunk, bad, bad mother,
now I hear your sweet quick complaint. It is lifted always

with laughing,
as leaves on the planes are kept fluttering by the movements of air.
And your rough bleached hair

and brown eye –
cast at an angle on your child's pennies, or the cat,
or Winnie the Pooh who pops up –

are full-blown
and big, blowsy with a rough independence. I like you,
my child likes you too. He says your name.

My Mother's Bathroom Armoury

Beehive proppers backcomb teasers
Pinpoint pluck of fearful tweezers
Leak of mouthwash morbid flavour
Dutch-cap dusted snap-shut cover
Cutting edge of lady-razor
Glint of sin and lure of danger
Woman's flesh a fading treasure
Braced for pain but honed for pleasure

Caked on flakes of failed concealer
Tell-tale cheeks of blusher-stealer
Crimson smear of lipstick wearer
Smile expander mouth preparer
Burning bleach a making-over
Smudged remains of caked mascara
Iron clamp of eyelash curler
Usual instruments of torture
Bath brimful of scented water
Mother's tricks will pass to daughter

This year next year sometime never

Part 2

"Violet,

before the surface of the lake slid over my head,
before my held breath eased its bubbles through water
and just before my arms recalled the butterfly stroke,
I like to think I saw you,
lifted a cabinet's velvet veil
to peep at you like a painted miniature of a loved one
shielded from light. You were a watercolour baby –
all pale skin, eyes like blue suns setting in the dark
and a mouth like a giggling blossom
learning to take the air."

---

what maria told me on monday morning

"– with our baby, in
immoral cohabitation:
i don't think that he'll make me his wife,
but i hope so. maybe.
i can't believe that everyone's opting for life,
including the bump, including the baby,
who appeared without warning
as a stripe on a stick.
i am not elegant enough to do this yet, anna.
i am not grown up enough.
i feel sick."

Where the baby isn't

At work, where the baby isn't, I fuss with
Tasks and repetitions and they lack salt. Then
I go home, do my crossword on the train,
Where the baby isn't, and walk back reading.
Rummage for the keys in the bag's last corner,
Where the baby isn't; go in, check for mail or
Notes from the hospital about the missing baby,
Then the aimless grazing of evening in the
Kitchen where the baby isn't. The computer
Has no baby though it's full of messages
About its coming and going and there's no baby
In the washing or the washing up and the
Bathroom is where the baby didn't and the
Bedroom is where the weight of its absence
Flattened me and where the baby won't sleep
And neither does my husband and the days,
The weeks, a year ahead resound with the
Nothing, where the baby isn't, and the
Whole wide shape of the world is a mirror
Reflecting where the baby isn't.

Laud in the Turning Leaves

Redder than a pound of fresh ground beef
and redder than the poison on a sprig of holly,
redder even than last night when, late
and thinking yourself finally pregnant,
you discovered you were redly not:

redder still, the sun this morning rises.

From your window, city towers make a glare
of glass like fine cosmetics counters –
this, the capital of lipstick. The river,
like a ruddy sheet of copper, blinks and blinks.

Already out there dripping sugar
in the carnival of it all, your husband
is a great candied apple of a man.
While he fancies a son like a sweet tooth,
back home everything pinks and rouges.

Griever, it's the scheme of certain maples in October
to immolate so slowly every person passing
seems like Moses, but not all fires
are trick façades for some divine communication.
You're not so much an arson as you are the crux
of family ardour. Lesser flames admire

the way you softly weep for tinder while you burn.

Child

She slept
  like a small child,
barely denting the sheets.
Life hummed inside her
        – a hungry ghost.
  Beauty is most exquisite
when fragile:
    eggshell, lily,
        a shoulder-blade's
          rise and crumple.

  Let nothing trouble this!
Dispel the alarms;
  day's whining light
  which catches
on glass and splits
        itself apart
  with colour; the someone
click-opening the door;
  each wakeful
      suggestion.

Nullipara

Concave am I, with mouth agape,
and you so vexed at my hollow curve.
Circumspect, you scan the room
and watch this space take shape, then snigger,
sock it to me, sucker-punch.
I'll stand my brave new ground,
cagey at your gesture to disaster,
shrinking from the prospect
of a pint-sized master.
I hoard my blood and milk in pots,
overflowing plastic beakers,
brimming cradles, sodden cots,
wrap my cave around me like a cape
and clutch eggs close like newborn babes.

Talisman

Were I to keep a dried seahorse at my breast like wives of fishermen wishing to coax milk flow I wonder if I'd hear an infant cry. Lactation enlivened by dead sealife worn as jewellery beautifully noosed and knocking at my sternum. The horse hangs limp and leaves a rash. Chestflesh turned to coral.

Were I to carry frogbones cut and carved into fertility sticks I secrete about my person perhaps I'd feel tiny fingers grab my thumb. Summon pink shell fingernails by holding old amphibian bones in my clothes. They fill my pockets and clackclack. I walk bandy-legged and leap to stifle sound.

Were I to look with any openness at the bloodclot creature babe in question I would see strange progeny. I'd see a bairn with a raisin face. Child, you are grape skins stretched over fishbones. The red and blue insides of wrists. Fragile underside of retracted snails, gracile and so pale I see through you.

You are crab claws unfurling into cabbage leaves. Fanning fine-veined limbs peeled from your core make me heartsore. I was once cleaved to you. We are now cleaved in two. I feel the cut too much. So I draw fleshtone tattoos on the bottom of my feet and press our soles together to fix a print in ink. When you walk you will make marks.

Grasshopper Warbler

Amongst the iris beds at Dimmingsdale
all May I waited,
sat out on the bow each evening
as day fell into the arms of night
and searched the twilight for your voice,
unpicking the dusk-song – for what?
A cricket, a mill wheel,
a girl spinning straw in her lonely tower?
I scanned the reedclumps and the meadowsweet
for your skulking creep, shy mouse-bird
fossicking in your secret world.

How those weeks seemed endless,
waiting too for the little creature that grew inside me
unseen, unheard, unknowable as you
in his private dark.
I was always listening, never unafraid.
I made fool's bargains with the fields:
keep jack-in-the-hedge flowering in an egg cup
and he would live;
see a kit – yes; four magpies – yes;
hear you, your song, your grasshopper song
to feel him trembling through me
like the wind through the reeds.

Nights I fretted you would never come,
the rushes alive with everything but you,
the moon waning too quickly into June.

I was raw, heart-bare, a shorn cornfield, willow stripped,
until that gloaming, sweet gloaming, weeks on,
when I heard you calling in the cut's half-light,
reeling and insistent as that tiny heartbeart.
Small bird, amongst the irises
I knelt and I wept.

I have a comfort house inside my body

I never knew that I had a special space inside my body
                   a comfort house
Warm, filled with music, fabrics, the big science project
                   of human mechanism
I never knew that I had a planet inside my body
Between the hardware of the arteries, bones,
                   cells, meats, and hormonal systems
                   collaborating, moving,
                   creating all possibilities
I never knew that in my life, there could be a life,
                   a process, from zero to sustainability
Many people say that it is normal, if you are a woman
                   it is ordinary
I never knew that I had the ability to share, give, carry on
                   between the gag and hassle
                   nicotine free
I never knew that I would welcome another human
                   to use my heart beat
                   and fall in love with towering enthusiasm
I never knew that I had patience
                   to wait for your appearance
I never knew that I had a heart that was big enough
                   for caring
I never knew that I was faithful
I never knew that I had a comfort house inside my body
                   and would develop it day by day,
                   to fit your growth and development

I never said sorry to you before
　　　　　　sorry, if that house was small-scale,
　　　　　　because I am tiny,
　　　　　　cute tummy
But I hope that you liked your old house
　　　　　　though it wasn't a castle
　　　　　　for a little prince like you
I hope that someday you will understand
　　　　　　there was a warm house inside my body
　　　　　　that I want you to come back inside it
　　　　　　to come home
If someday the world out there is too barbarous for you.

Bambino

We are walking inside the Colosseum
looking at the ruin of civilization
Sometimes I stop my steps
caressing you inside my stomach
       and telling you about the poetic histories
We are not travellers like Byron in Rome was
but I am trying to make you comfortable
and hoping you are not too tired
because I love walking
       down, up, down from the bus
You are so cool, so calm inside my belly
Sometimes we are dancing together
       in the Centro Storico Napoli
just to see the life, culture-set, Roman
Sometimes we are enjoying gelato Fior di Latte
       and because we are both happy
       you are kicking me once again
Sometimes I just pray: for you, for us, our family
       in Piazza Bellini
Sometimes we are buying some Limoncello
       for your dad and my husband
Sometimes you are very calm when I am crying in my bed
trying to write poems
       and I know that you are my reason for life
       after hearing your heart rate for a hundred years

Please forgive our silliness

Cercare Dio
Il mio bambino

We
are
the children too.

The Steps

And this is where it begins, love –
you and I, alone one last time in the slaty night,
the smell of you like Autumn, soil and bonfire,
that November the fourth feeling inside us.
There can be no truer wedding than this:
your bare hand in mine, my body winded
with pain, as you lead me to the car, to the
soon life. And we are frightened, so frightened –

Who will we be when we come back?
Will we remember ourselves?
Will we still touch each other's faces
in the darkness, the white noise of night
spilling over us, and believe there is nothing
we could not know or love?

Part 3

The Tempest

Six floors up, the hospital window
frames rage across the bay.
Out I peer at lightning spears
and surging greys. I cannot
hear trouble outside or beyond

the sound of cow –
"Noise won't help," the midwife mutters
and quits my stall. She disapproves
of the *mmmooooooooooooo*

which escapes,
trails the corridor
and, reaching the office,
insists she enter
a lonely note in my hospital file.

Of course, I imagine the entry
and scene. Star of my Act, I watch
my husband, who watches. Composed.
I say, "If it's a boy, we'll call him Prospero."
He says, "We know she's a girl. We agreed

on Grace."
I bellow, and bellow again
when he repeats,
"We agreed."
I should have agreed

to a different part: not *The Cow*
and not *The Labourer*.

I want to charge
at the man who plays
The Expectant Father.

Instead, all fours on the bed,
urgent and mooing, I struggle
for Grace –

                  who emerges.
Tempest-triumphant, she
pumps her fists. And roars.

Fontanelle

It throbbed like a slow naked heart, the soft
part of you your skull hadn't welcomed
in its cradle of bone. I poured water
over your strips of old-man's hair
hardly daring to touch it.

Sixteen years on I watch you
header footballs into a net,
and with each rush of air, each thump,
feel the weight of your head again, hear
the midwife's voice – *Be careful of that bit.*

Collage

The day opens and closes about us like scissors. They take you away.
They bring you back. You have a lump of plastic stuck into your hand.
They slit holes for your eyes. You look at me

like liver looks at me, like heart. You are familiar as innards.
In strip-light I clean your first shit. I'm not sure I do it right.
It sticks to me like funeral silk.

They place us in a rectangle, neatly-cut. Right-angular.
Our limbs bleed like permanent ink through paper. Corridors echo
snip, snip, snip. We are soft as roe. There is a window

guillotined into the wall. I scoop you up like a clod.
The world outside is a smudge. We look out at the shapes
a city makes. On the far hill, the sky is furred; frayed with rain.

You have such weight. You have the living scent of clay.

When Six O'clock Comes and Another Day has Passed

the baby who cannot speak, speaks to me.
When the sun has risen and set over the same dishes
and the predicted weather is white cloud,
the baby steadies her head which is the head of a drunk's
and holds me with her blue eyes,
eyes which have so recently surfed through womb-swell,
and all at once we stop half-heartedly row, rowing
our boat and see each other clear
in the television's orange glow. She regards me,
the baby who does not know a television from a table lamp,
the baby, who is so heavy with other people's hopes
she has no body to call her own,
the baby who is forever being shifted, rearranged,
whose hands must be unfurled and wiped with cotton wool,
whose scalp must be combed of cradle cap,
the baby who has exactly no memories
softens her face in the early evening light and says I understand.

Cocoon

The day butterflies broke free from my body
they unrolled me like a paper-thin cocoon,

pulled tightly with silk fingers,
held me up to the light and saw right through me.

They fold me differently each day:
sometimes a hat, sometimes a boat.

At sundown they turn back my corners,
press me flat, but the creases remain.

Once they cut me into a child's snowflake;
that night the holes in my body leaked dark onto the bed.

There are versions of me in magazines, glossy sheets
that mock my worn parchment until its corners curl.

Each morning I try to draw myself a mouth
but the lines blur, bleed my lips to buttons;

sometimes I romanticise myself into letters
from imagined lovers who run their ink-stained fingers

over my yellowed skin as if it were lined with gold.
One day I will fold myself into a bird.

The light draws me like a moth in winter
until the edges of me are singed black.

I am afraid of windy days and hold on tightly
to my children's paperweight arms.

DIY

Don't fret about the damp patch
under the window; the baby won't mind.

She'll not bother her head
about the lagging in the roof-space.

The bare floorboards that bring
the sound of your footsteps

will do her just fine, that crack
in the ceiling will be her first pattern.

She won't lose any sleep over
the missing loft ladder,

the crazed toilet bowl, the stubborn cold tap,
that creosote spilling through the fence.

Listen. Already she outgrows her prison,
drums her heels against its walls,

turns turtle, butts her head, blinks,
opens and closes her mouth.

Sit down, pick up your guitar
and sing to her.

The New Mothers

They have mastered the buggy –
they understand the awkward catch,
what force of pressure makes it give.
They wheel with confidence, more
confidence, they wheel through afternoons
of amnesiac light, through mornings
loud with rain and evenings when
the sky is soothed to pink, thinking of
the secrets recently unshelled, the ones
their mothers kept so long, the bloody
songs of sealed rooms which day by day
grow faint and fainter still.
They pass by women being wheeled,
women sinking in their chairs who once
(can it be true?) sat small and snug
in carriage prams. Swelling women
pass by too, manoeuvring their mounds
they seem as far removed as first year girls
to sixth formers. And of course
they pass their kind, in cafés, parks –
half smiles, shy, as if they saw the nipples weep
inside each other's clothes. Another cup of tea;
they pause and redirect their gaze away,
beyond the complicated child they've made,
beyond the blurred pedestrians to girls
in skinny jeans, remembering how (again
impossibly) they were those girls,
the Matryoshka trick that had them

for a minute spot-lit, arms raised
to glorify the tiny hours, sweat glittering
their foreheads – white light, noise –
and years away, unreachable through dance floor mist,
babies with wet mouths feeding in the dark.

Paul Cézanne – Hortense Breast Feeding Paul (1872)

Hortense dozing,
  dreaming, the contents
of her content
  hidden from us,
dreaming, dozing
  in a long tradition,
Isis nursing Horus,
  Memling's nursing Mary,
Corot's breastfeeding mother,
  but the painting,

like Hortense,
  is turned away from
this knowledge,
  neither sacred nor sexy.
Hortense's closed eyes
  do not return a gaze,
so do not confirm
  anything we think we know
about mothers, breasts or babies.
  Soft curves

———————

of pillow and bedding
  are breast-like, body-like,
echoing Hortense.
  And the paint is quiet,
a sleepy 'nothing to see here' hum
  done quickly.
The viewer is not required.
  Everyone knows what they know
and need to know: Hortense
  is breastfeeding Paul.

CLARE POLLARD

Emmanuel

Herod, the king, in his raging,
Charged he hath this day
His men of might, in his own sight,
All young children to slay.

The Coventry Carol

I woke because I thought he was awake,
but he's not awake now I'm awake
and the street is not awake –
it has been held and shushed by ice.

The frost is breath on a looking-glass;
the pulse of Christmas lights
makes the shadows move
as his eyelids move,

but his shriek gouged like a nail
and he thrashes: something
has injured sleep, something
I won't let happen is happening.

In the day he is blithe; all light.
Christ was a child, famously.
Poor lamb, how the whole dark world
must have squatted above his crib.

Too absurd to think of God
in a flyspeck beast, oblivious
to itself; his burp and drool;
the wet gold blaze of his raised bum.

Did Jesus have these meat-sleeves,
this snodgy nose, the welts
on the ball-sack; could he really be
so innocent? Poor Mary fled

the darkness her own son uttered,
clutching her swaddled love
through Egypt; cave after cave.
To be blessed is a kind of terror.

Part 4

The Child Jesus

My scarred child is not 'boisterous'
like one of the famously daredevil
hanging from trees boys,
three to a motorbike –
he does recycling club, Bengali cookery,
at school he is everyone's pet. When he gets angry
he puts on an apron and makes biscuits
(rosewater, cardamon, butter, flour).
He is our pet because
we rely on his sacrifices:
last in the queue, first to surrender
with no thought of ever winning –
he knows better than that,
is cynical on the subject of competition,
won't bother with raffles or speculation
on the number of jelly beans;
he is covered in scars.

His little brother would lash out
and wouldn't stop until he drew blood –
the dashes on his skin show up in the sun,
hyphenated scratches where a nail broke
on his face. I remember hitting a wall
when I lost my temper with him once,
I don't remember why.
He was there when I threw a kettle
and a laptop across the kitchen
at his father.

He was there when I wasn't.
Something about living with him
brought out our human worst.
I think our worst thing
was asking him to forgive us,
all the time, not stopping until he did.
Sitting in a row on the sofa, praising his baking.

Daughters

They're phantoms, nameless, but
they make their presence felt.

The one who sings *Summertime*
in the bathroom leaves taps running,

vanilla-scent lingering in the steam.
My earrings, tights, lipsticks vanish;

wine stains bloom on carpets.
5 a.m., there's one on the doorstep,

no key – sits with head in hands,
nauseous; vodka, I guess, flashbacks

to some boy's tongue in her mouth;
feet blistered, handbag spitting sequins.

She's dark, like me, but the fair ones
are like the dads they might have had –

the politics student from Leicester or
that Swedish physiotherapist on Kos.

Sometimes snatches of their laughter
seep downstairs – I imagine them

sprawled on the youngest one's bed,
painting each other's nails purple –

but often they squabble, their voices
raw and shrill as hungry crows.

When we all bleed on the same day,
the house shudders from banged doors.

In my mirror the singing one stands
behind me, combs her long wet hair –

meets my eyes for a few seconds,
then stares straight through me.

Ten

The worksheet we've been given
requires us to fill in
this blank:

'In ten years I will be __ years old.'

In ten years I will look up to his face
instead of down; his cheeks will be rough
with blond stubble.

Today his red moods
swirl inside his chest. Blue blotches sketch
a path down my leg, drawn by the kicks
of his hiking boots. The one below

my knee has faded to the colour
his eyelids turned
as the forceps ripped him from water to air.

I'd settled into flat relief, breathing
the scent of his unwashed newborn skin,

until he craved space, preferred bottles to breast,
his own cot to my bed. At two years old
he could not speak,

but now he is ten, made of murmurs, shouts,
and gabbles, facts about videogames, gadgets.

He can program machines but can't translate
what his body means with words. He whispers
"I'm a ghost", and lets go. Then he's my baby again.

Manboy

My skanky virgin boy sixteen
cleans teeth   *for ten minutes*

Sticks cotton bud in ears
waggles about   *finds gold*

Squeezes zits and
with Lynx Africa   *bogan pheromones*

under his arms
goes to meet his maker

the virgin queen   *out of Africa indeed*

into the realm of
stink finger
knocked teeth and   *oops, did I do that?*

Yes you did   Manboy
now come and eat your Wheaties

Medea's Farewell

You look at me with fishbowl eyes, swimming
pleas for mercy. And how could I resist
those smiles that brim so full of kidding
jokes and tiny, tombstone teeth I kissed
the day they broke through gums and bit
my nipple that wept thimblefuls of blood
and milk onto your pouting lips. I'm split
in two over this. You cut me up with love
but look how I have gone all soft and baulk
at my own mind. The goddess in me
will not let this yellow-livered belly-talk
smother her resolve. Come on, banshee!
Bite me once, I've nothing left to lose.
Go in children, it's bedtime. To the noose!

Daughters

Look to your daughters, careful parents,
for they are numerous in nature:
blue-eyed boys with new hearts that need tending.
These boys are keen to love, and your daughters
will spend long hours bending over them.
Your daughters' hair will fall on their unworthy faces.
Your daughters' ecstatic lips will make them grow.
Your daughters will water them,
and your daughters will come in from the garden wild-eyed,
and you will have to let your daughters go again,
back to the boys, though you know
how your daughters will be cut
on the opening rose of them.

Once I Was Telling You, My Daughter

Once I was telling you, my daughter, when the spring is coming,
        it is time for all the flowers to wake up and breathe
Once I was reminding you about time that is always clocking,
        tic-tac tic-tac
        at the same moment you give your heart up
        give your hope up
        the time will still be clocking
Once I was sitting in our family room, my daughter,
watching you from my sights that don't have a distance
        missing you so much
        whispering that your heart was fine
Once I was loving you, my daughter,
        hoping you would remember the key of loving
        is being able to be giving
Once I was starting my day in the garden in our little white house,
        and suddenly I realized that you are strong,
        because on the day you were born
        I stole wings from the smiley angel
Once I was closing my eyes, murmuring short words like *smile*
        and *you'll be fine*
        holding on to little things
        that deserve to be heard, to be considered,
Are you listening, my daughter?
            You might be foolish, at risk, but –
            there is no other way to taste life,
            and there is no reason
            not to be a lover

While I am telling you this, my daughter,
I am hoping that you dare to see anything in front of you
while having a good heart for everything behind you
I know you will do it all, my daughter,

Your wings might be broken,
but your heart is living to be a weapon.

Monopoly

Almost bankrupt and only recently released from jail,
she owes her ten year old
four hundred quid in rent
for landing on his new hotel in Bond Street.
He owns most of the West End
and several public utilities.
She pleads poverty. He points out
she could give him Leicester Square
and they could come to some arrangement
over her arrears. She thinks how

this is what capitalism does to children –
brutalises them, makes them worship
five-hundred pound notes, little red boxes,
encourages them to sniff out the weak
and charge them exorbitant rent,
rob them blind, make them beg.
She watches his fingers fatten on his stash

and she tells him, *No.* She'll take her chances,
and hangs onto Leicester Square. She likes
the Japanese men with their cameras,
their perfect hair, their busy hands,
she likes the pigeon shit, the café
with the gilt-framed photo of the Queen
where the waiter gives her extra chocolate
on her cappuccino, no favours asked.

Goddess

I love a bare world like the world I strode with my boy.
I held his hand. I said, "This is a wall of wind." I pitched

the words over the wall, but the wind-whirr deafened him.
His walk was a wrestle. The wan sky was his twin.

His father beckoned him to the swings
and the world grew barer. My son's love is a burden,

the Oedipal beat, beat, beat of his fist on his
father's tee-shirted chest. I see

that his leaving will repeat itself; I will let him leave.
And I love a bare world.

Once my husband declared me a goddess
of destruction. I approved of that view. I view

myself that way, too: Queen of an Uninhabited Planet.
I tread on moon-rubble. Dust circles my knees.

My dress is Belgian deconstructionist. I am barefoot and regal
and unadorned but for the anklet from the morgue.

I am mother to all that is bare, all that is gone
for I have expected the bare world all along.

The End of Envy

The end of envy
Is a staircase in midair.

From there,
There is nothing to want,

But there is wind to love.
I miss what the wind bent,

But I'm used to the bare world.

When I was sentenced to the stairs
For eternity, I didn't know

I would climb them pregnant,
Or ill, or with the aim of soothing a cry

That would reappear
As soon as I was at the bottom.

In a way I am happy here on the stairs,
For the end of envy

Is the end of desire, the end of the edifice,
But not of elevation.

The Night You Were Born

November 27th, a month before me, all the lights
in the Black Country out for the evening,

Wren's Nest tucked under a blanket of darkness,
mithered only by the fog-beams of your dad's van

as it sped to the hospital. In the back, the dog,
snuffling in her bed of tools and woodshavings.

In the front, your mom, panting on the turns,
her frightened moon face waning at the window.

I think about that night when I doze, heavy
with our son, in the snow-soft hours.

What it would have been to have seen you, pushed
howling, from that red tent of legs,

the first word on the page of our story.
I press myself against you in the darkness, listen

for your murmur as he moves inside me. Oh love,
I can almost hear it now: that first cry –

a raw thread of sound spooling through Winter
to stitch our lives together.

Acknowledgements

'On Returning a Child To Her Mother at the Natural History Museum', by Kathryn Maris, appeared first in *Poetry London* and then in *God Loves You* (Seren, 2013). Reprinted with kind permission from Seren.

'National Moth Night', by Richard O'Brien, was first published in his debut pamphlet *your own devices* (tall-lighthouse, 2009).

'Madame de Grignan Writes to the Marquise', by Laura Chalar, has previously been published in *Rain Dog* magazine, *Legal Studies Forum* and *Poemeleon*.

'Poem for Virgin Starfish', by Peter LaBerge, previously appeared in Issue Two of *Winter Tangerine Review*.

'Violet' was first published in Camellia Stafford's first collection, *Letters to the Sky* (Salt, 2013).

'Laud in the Turning Leaves', by George David Clark, was originally published as 'Reveille in Red' in the journal *Willow Springs*, 68 (2011).

'Grasshopper Warbler', by Liz Berry, was first published in *Poetry Review*.

'Fontanelle', by Catherine Smith, was first published in *Lip* (Smith/Doorstop, 2008).

'When Six O'clock Comes and Another Day has Passed', by Kathryn Simmonds, was first published in *The North* and subsequently in *The Forward Book of Poetry 2013* and *The Visitations* (Seren, 2013).

'DIY', by Carole Bromley, previously appeared in *Poetry News* and her collection *A Guided Tour of the Ice House* (Smith/Doorstop, 2011).

'The New Mothers', by Kathryn Simmonds, was first published in *Poetry London* and then in *The Visitations* (Seren, 2013).

'Daughters', by Catherine Smith, was first published in the *Rialto* in 2010.

'Monopoly', by Catherine Smith, was first published in *The Butcher's Hands* (Smith/Doorstop, 2003).

'Goddess', by Kathryn Maris, was first published in the *Cimarron Review* before appearing on *Poetry Daily* and then in *The Book of Jobs* (Four Way Books, 2006).

'The End of Envy', by Kathryn Maris, previously appeared in the magazine *Ploughshares* and then in *The Book of Jobs* (Four Way Books, 2006).

'The Night You Were Born', by Liz Berry, was first published in *Ambit*.

About the poets

Deborah Alma teaches at the University of Worcester and works with people with dementia and at the end of their lives using poetry. Her first pamphlet is *True Tales of the Countryside* (Emma Press, 2015) and she is the editor of *The Emergency Poet: An Anti-Stress Poetry Anthology* (Michael O'Mara Books, 2015). She is half-Indian and lives in Powys.

Stephanie Arsoska lives on the east coast of Scotland with her husband and two children. She has been commended in competitions and has had work published with *Prole*, Mother's Milk Books, Iron Press, *Magma*, *Ink Sweat & Tears*, *Nutshell & Nuggets*, *The Open Mouse* and *Lighthouse*.

Liz Berry was born in the Black Country and lives in Birmingham with her family. Her debut collection, *Black Country* (Chatto & Windus, 2014), was a Poetry Book Society Recommendation, received a Somerset Maugham Award, won the Geoffrey Faber Memorial Prize and the Forward Prize for Best First Collection 2014.

Sara Boyes has contributed poems to a number of anthologies, including *Images of Women* and *Soul Feathers,* and has also produced two collections, *Kite* and *Wildflowers* (Stride, 1989 and 1993), and a pamphlet, *Black Flame* (Hearing Eye, 2005). In a former life she worked in theatre, writing and acting in plays. She now teaches creative writing.

Carole Bromley has two pamphlets and two collections with Smith/Doorstop, the most recent being *The Stonegate Devil* (2015). They will publish her first collection for children, *Blast Off!*, in spring 2017.

Laura Chalar was born in Montevideo, Uruguay, where she trained as a lawyer. She is the author of six books, including a poetry collection, *Midnight at the Law Firm* (Coal City Press, 2015). She has published numerous translations from and into Spanish (including works by Jane Austen and Mary Wollstonecraft), as well as writing for children.

George David Clark teaches poetry at Valparaiso University. His most recent poems can be found in new issues of *Alaska Quarterly Review*, *FIELD*, *The Missouri Review*, *The Southwest Review*, *The Yale Review* and elsewhere. He lives in Indiana with his wife and their two young children.

Flora de Falbe was a Foyle Young Poet in 2011 and 2012 and has read at events including the Ledbury Festival and Chelsea Fringe. Her work has bee published in *CAKE*, *Rising* and an anthology by Eyewear Publishing.

Kate Garrett is the founding editor of Three Drops Press and the web journal *Picaroon Poetry*. Her work has been widely published online and in print, and her pamphlet *The Density of Salt* (Indigo Dreams, 2016) was longlisted for a Saboteur Award in 2016. Her next pamphlet, *You've never seen a doomsday like it*, is forthcoming from Indigo Dreams in 2017.

Hilary Gilmore was raised in the Blue Mountains outside Sydney, and returned there in 2012 after eleven years living in Britain and Eastern Europe. Her professional life concerns the history, cultures and physical poetry of material things, especially clothing. She has published extensively in this field.

Melinda Kallasmae lives in country Victoria, Australia, with her sons and their cats. Her poems have been published in Australian anthologies and magazines including *The Australian Writer*, *Verandah* and *Tamba*.

David Kennedy lives and writes in Sheffield. He has published three collections with Salt, most recently *The Devil's Bookshop* (2007). He has also published pamphlets with Oyster Catcher and Rack Press.

Anna Kirk is from Northumberland. She has studied at both UCL and Royal Holloway and now works at Slightly Foxed, an independent publisher and literary magazine.

Anna Kisby is a Devon-based poet and mother of three, widely published in magazines and anthologies. In 2016 she won the Proms Poetry Competition, the Havant Poetry Competition and was commended in the Faber New Poets Scheme.

Peter LaBerge is the author of two chapbooks: *Makeshift Cathedral* (YesYes Books, 2017) and *Hook* (Sibling Rivalry Press, 2015). His work appears in *Beloit Poetry Journal, Best New Poets, Harvard Review, Indiana Review, Iowa Review, Pleiades* and *Tin House*. He is editor-in-chief of *The Adroit Journal* and a student at the University of Pennsylvania.

Eve Lacey is from Brighton and lives in Cambridge, where she works as a librarian. She is the editor of *Furies*, an anthology of contemporary women's poetry published by For Books' Sake in 2014, and *The Emma Press Anthology of the Sea* (2016).

Anna Leader has published a novel, *Tentative*, and a collection of poetry, *Squeak Like Dolls*, and was the joint first-place winner of the Stephen Spender Prize for Poetry in Translation in 2013.

Marena Lear was born in Havana, but has lived most of her life in different parts of the Pacific Northwest of the U.S., land of pine trees, Nirvana, and delicious coffee. She is currently an MA student at the University of East Anglia. This is her first publication.

Katherine Lockton is co-editor of the *South Bank Poetry* magazine. Her poetry has appeared in numerous journals and magazines including *Magma, Rising, Northwords Now, Brittle Star, The Dark Horse* and *The Morning Star*. She has performed at venues such as The Torriano Meeting House, The Troubadour, Calder's Theatre and the Poetry Café.

Rachel Long is an alumna of the 2015-16 Jerwood/Arvon Mentorship scheme. She is Assistant Tutor on the Barbican Young Poets programme and leads Octavia, a poetry collective for Women of Colour, housed at Southbank Centre.

Julie Maclean is the author of *To Have to Follow* (Indigo Dream, 2016), *Kiss of the Viking* (Poetry Salzburg, 2014) and *When I saw Jimi* (Indigo Dreams, 2013), which won the Geoff Stevens Poetry Prize after being shortlisted for the Crashaw Prize (Salt). Her chapbook *Lips That Did* is due in 2017 with Dancing Girl Press. www.juliemacleanwriter.com

Ikhda Ayuning Maharsi is a multicultural poet and a big fan of her two young children. Living in France and now working as an educational assistant, Ikhda believes that the world is a huge playground. Her debut poetry pamphlet, *Ikhda by Ikhda*, was published by the Emma Press in 2014. Characters and landscapes are a constant source of inspiration for her.

Kathryn Maris is a poet from New York City who has lived in London since 1999. She is the author of two collections, *The Book of Jobs* (2006) and *God Loves You* (2013). Her poems have appeared in anthologies including *Best British Poetry 2012* and the *Oxford Poets Anthology*. She teaches creative writing for the Poetry School and the Arvon Foundation.

Richard O'Brien's second pamphlet, *The Emmores*, was published by the Emma Press in 2014 and *A Bloody Mess* followed from Valley Press in 2015. His work has featured in *Oxford Poetry, Poetry London,* and *The Best British Poetry 2013.* He is working on a Midlands3Cities-funded PhD on Shakespeare and the development of verse drama at the University of Birmingham.

Clare Pollard's new translation of *Ovid's Heroines* (Bloodaxe, 2013) has toured as a one-woman show with Jaybird Live Literature. Her fifth collection, about motherhood, will be *Incarnation* (Bloodaxe, 2017). Her website is www.clarepollard.com

Jacqueline Saphra's collection *The Kitchen of Lovely Contraptions* (flipped eye) was nominated for the Aldeburgh First Collection Prize. Her Saboteur award-winning pamphlet *If I Lay On My Back I Saw Nothing But Naked Women* was published by the Emma Press in 2014 and her next collection, *All My Mad Mothers,* is due from Nine Arches Press in 2017.

Kathryn Simmonds has published two poetry collections with Seren: *Sunday at the Skin Launderette* (2008) and *The Visitations* (2013). Her first novel, *Love and Fallout,* will be published by Seren in June 2014. She is currently poet-in-residence at the Charles Causley Trust in Launceston, Cornwall.

Lavinia Singer won the Newdigate Prize at Oxford in 2010. She completed her Creative Writing MA at Royal Holloway in 2012 and is co-editor of *Oxford Poetry.* She currently works at Enitharmon Press, teaches Old English and sells ice cream at the Southbank Centre.

Catherine Smith was one of the Poetry Book Society's Next Generation Poets in 2004. Twice short-listed in the Forward Prizes, her latest publication is *The New Cockaigne* (Frogmore Press) – a pamphlet-length surreal, supernatural poem described by Ros Barber as 'A fascinating satire on how totalitarian thought processes imprison us all.'

Camellia Stafford was born in Warwickshire. She read English Literature at King's College London and has an Art History MA from The Courtauld Institute of Art. Her debut poetry collection *Letters to the Sky* is published by Salt. Her poems have appeared in *Oxford Poetry*, *Magma* and *Best British Poetry 2013*.

Megan Watkins' work has been published by *The Echo Room*, *Morning Star*, *Transom*, *Smiths Knoll*, *Magma*, *Tears in the Fence* and other extremely good publications. Her children are 9 and 7 years old, she started writing poetry when they were little because it is short and all you need is a notebook.

About the editors

Rachel Piercey is a poet and editor who also writes for children. Her poems have appeared in magazines including *Magma*, *The Rialto*, *Poems In Which*, *Butcher's Dog* and *The Poetry Review* and she has two pamphlets with the Emma Press, *The Flower and the Plough* and *Rivers Wanted*.

Emma Wright studied Classics at Brasenose College, Oxford. She worked in ebook production at Orion Publishing Group before leaving to set up the Emma Press in 2012. She lives in Birmingham.

THE EMMA PRESS

small press, big dreams

The Emma Press is an independent publisher dedicated to producing beautiful, thought-provoking books. It was founded in 2012 by Emma Wright in Winnersh, UK, and was shortlisted for the Michael Marks Award for Poetry Pamphlet Publishers in 2014, 2015 and 2016.

Our current publishing programme features a mixture of themed poetry anthologies and single-author poetry and prose pamphlets, with an ongoing engagement with the works of the Roman poet Ovid. We publish books which excite us, and we are often on the lookout for new writing.

Sign up to the monthly Emma Press newsletter to hear about all our events and publications, as well as upcoming calls for submissions. All of our books are available to buy from our online shop, at the Prince's Trust Tomorrow's Store in London, and in all good bookshops.

theemmapress.com
emmavalleypress.blogspot.co.uk

ALSO FROM THE EMMA PRESS

THE EMMA PRESS ANTHOLOGY OF AGE

Edited by Sarah Hesketh
RRP £10 / ISBN 978-1-910139-31-8

The Emma Press Anthology of Age is a collection of poems which
challenge, celebrate and give age a voice, finding humour amidst
heartbreak and comfort within pain.

HOMESICKNESS AND EXILE

POEMS ABOUT LONGING AND BELONGING

Edited by Rachel Piercey and Emma Wright
RRP £10 / ISBN 978-1-910139-02-8

How does it feel to be a foreigner? Can you choose where you call
home? *Homesickness and Exile* is a collection of poems about the
fundamental human need to belong to a place.

ALSO FROM THE EMMA PRESS

MALKIN, by Camille Ralphs

RRP £5 / ISBN 978-1-910139-30-1

Malkin brims and bubbles with the voices of those accused in the
Pendle Witch Trials of 1612. Thirteen men and women – speaking
across the centuries via Ralphs' heady use of free spelling – plead,
boast and confess, immersing the reader in this charged and
dangerous time in history.

SLOW THINGS: POEMS ABOUT SLOW THINGS

Edited by Rachel Piercey and Emma Wright

RRP £10 / ISBN 978-1-910139-16-5

Slow walks, slow thoughts and slow afternoons in the sun provide
inspiration for the poets in *Slow Things*, an anthology which
celebrates taking life at a leisurely pace and existing in the present.

ALSO FROM THE EMMA PRESS

GOOSE FAIR NIGHT, by Kathy Pimlott

With an introduction by Clare Pollard

RRP £6.50 / ISBN 978-1-910139-35-6

A generous, jellied feast of a book, full of sharp-eyed yet tender details about friendship, family and familiarity.

DISSOLVE TO: L.A. by James Trevelyan

RRP £5 / ISBN 978-1-910139-37-0

What does it mean to die in a movie scene? To exist on the peripheries? Trevelyan takes twelve cult action films of the 1980s and 90s and gives life where it was extinguished too early.